MY FIRS

COLORING BOOK

belongs to: _____

ELEPHANT

GIRAFFE

HIPPO

FROG

SEAL

PARROT

CROCODILE

DEER

COW

WHALE

SHEEP

PENGUIN

monkey

OWL

Bunny

TORTOISE

KANGAROO

PEACOCK

HEDGEHOG

TOUCAN

PANDA

MEERKAT

MOOSE

BEAVER

DONKEY

LEOPARD

GOAT

OTTER

HUMMINGBIRD

LEMUR

GOOSE

PORCUPINEFISH

CATERPILLAR

PLATYPUS

GUINEA PIG

DRAGONFLY

GRASSHOPPER

STARFISH

RACCOON

BUFFALO

SHRIMP

PELICAN

BAT

EAGLE

WILD BOAR

PHEASANT

HYENA

AXOLOTL

MOLE